Original title:
December's Joyful Chill

Copyright © 2024 Creative Arts Management OÜ
All rights reserved.

Author: Dean Whitmore
ISBN HARDBACK: 978-9916-90-904-1
ISBN PAPERBACK: 978-9916-90-905-8

Embracing the Frost

The ground wears a blanket of white,
Snowmen wobble, a comical sight.
With mittens on hands and hats askew,
We tumble and slip, but laugh, it's true.

Sledding down hills, it's a wild spree,
Trees shiver in laughter, just like me.
With cheeks rosy red, we penguin slide,
In a frosty wonderland, we take pride.

Sparkling Nights

Under the stars, the snowflakes dance,
With twinkling lights, we take a chance.
Flip-flops in winter, just watch us go,
As we trip on the ice, it's quite the show!

Hot cocoa spills, a comedic plot,
With marshmallows flying, oh, what a lot!
We gather around, share laughter and cheer,
In this chilly season, there's joy to revere.

Cocoa Dreams

Warm mugs in hand, we sit by the fire,
Each sip seems to lift us higher.
With whipped cream clouds bobbing around,
Sipping our cocoa, giggles abound.

Sugar rush hits, we bounce and sway,
Juggling our cups in a clumsy display.
Cocoa dreams drift in a frothy sea,
With friends by my side, there's no better glee.

Twinkling Lights

Strings of colors, bright as the moon,
Decorate our homes with a merry tune.
Wobbling on ladders, what could go wrong?
As a star falls down, we burst into song!

Neighbors peeking out, with curious eyes,
As we hang mistletoe, amidst fits of sighs.
Each bulb a giggle, each sparkle a grin,
Under twinkling lights, the fun can begin.

The Call of Winter

Snowflakes tumble, dancing high,
Hot cocoa calls, oh my, oh my!
Socks upon socks, a fashion fright,
Bundled up, we shiver with delight.

Snowball fights in the chilly air,
A snowman grins, without a care.
Laughter echoes, until we fall,
'Tis the season for fun after all!

Warmth in the White

Hot hands grasping a steaming mug,
While outside, a snowball's a snug bug.
Fluffy hats and mittens too,
In this wild winter, we all pursue.

The fire crackles, the popcorn pops,
Everyone laughing, never stops.
Pajamas cozy, but who can tell?
We're just trying to avoid a spill!

Cold Moonlit Serenade

The moon hangs low, a silver glow,
We prance like penguins, don't you know?
Ice skates squeak, the feelings rise,
As we twirl 'neath winter skies.

A slip and slide, a tumble here,
Laughter rings, we shed a tear.
A frosty ballet, oh what a sight,
Who knew freezing could feel so light!

Frosted Whispers of Joy

Whispers of snowflakes on my nose,
Tickling my cheeks, a chilly dose.
Wrapping up tight, oh what a sight,
Can't find my boots, it's quite a plight!

Sledding down hills, we race and cheer,
Until someone's stuck, oh dear, oh dear!
Hot tea in hand, we gather near,
In this frosty fun, we have no fear!

Radiant Winter Mornings

Pajamas piled upon my chair,
Socks mismatched beyond compare.
Hot cocoa spills, a marshmallow float,
Chasing snowflakes on my coat.

Frost on windows, art so bright,
Puppies prance in pure delight.
With every nibble, crumbs align,
Cookies vanish, oh divine!

Frosty Footprints

Boots that squish and squeak a tune,
Sliding past the icy spoon.
Snowballs launched with giggly cries,
Laughter echoes 'neath gray skies.

Little ones, their cheeks aglow,
Making angels in the snow.
With each slip, a hearty laugh,
Bounding back, we take a gaff.

The Beauty of Stillness

Chill settles down as the sun goes low,
Sipping tea while fires glow.
Candles flicker, shadows play,
Mittens mingle in dismay.

Puppy snuggled, dreaming deep,
Snoring softly, no need for sleep.
Each quiet moment whispers cheer,
Warmth and laughter gather near.

Mirth in the Air

Hats too big and scarves that twist,
Snowflakes dance, we can't resist.
Gingerbread men with silly grins,
Poking fun at chubby chins.

Tickled toes in fluffy socks,
Snowmen dressed in funny frocks.
With each gust the giggles grow,
In this season, joy's aglow.

Whispers of Winter's Embrace

Snowflakes laugh as they twirl down,
Children chase like a playful hound.
Sleds zoom by, a sledding spree,
Hot cocoa spills for all to see.

The snowman grins with a silly hat,
While kids have a snowball chat.
Frosty the snowman cracks a joke,
Melting away, he's still no bloke.

Frosty Dances of Delight

Snowflakes shimmy and shake with glee,
While trees dress up for the holiday tea.
Elves in the park put on a show,
Jingle bells ring as the joy flows.

Breaths turn to clouds in the frosty air,
As laughter bounces everywhere.
Ice skating slips with a cheeky grin,
'Til someone falls, and the giggles begin.

Icicles of Laughter

Icicles hang like an old man's beard,
While snowflakes dance, the children cheered.
A puppy crashes into the snow,
With a wag of his tail, he steals the show.

Giggling loudly, they all take a fall,
Rolling around in a frosty sprawl.
Chasing snowflakes, the fun never ends,
With every slip, we make more friends.

The Chill of Cheerful Nights

The moon giggles as shadows play,
Frolicking critters at the end of day.
Hot chocolate spills, cocoa mustache,
As marshmallows dance in a sugary splash.

Nibbling cookies while tummies ache,
Silly stories around the lake.
While blankets wrap us in a cozy hug,
We know it's the laughter that keeps us snug.

The Magic of Silent Snowfall

Snowflakes twirl in graceful flights,
Dancing down like tiny lights.
They land on hats and on our hair,
We laugh and slip, without a care.

A snowman tilts, with carrot nose,
His lopsided smile is how it goes!
He wobbles when the kids pass by,
Like a tipsy friend who won't say goodbye.

Ember Glows and Frost-kissed Noses

Fires crackle, warmth we seek,
But marshmallows, oh, how they squeak!
They pop and hop, it's quite a show,
While frosty noses start to glow.

Hot chocolate spills, a sweet delight,
As giggles fill the winter night.
But watch your chin, it's quite a test,
For whipped cream hats are simply the best!

Warm Hugs Under Glistening Stars

Bundled tight, we hug so bold,
Giggling under stars like gold.
The air is crisp, the jokes are quick,
As snowflakes land, we all do a kick.

Laughter echoes through the night,
With every twist, a pure delight.
We dance around, like silly fools,
While snowmen clap, breaking the rules.

Dancing Shadows of Frosted Mornings

Morning light on frost reveals,
Shadows dancing, oh what deals!
With boots that squeak, we prance ahead,
While icy winds tickle instead.

Pigeons hop in search of bread,
While snowflakes land upon our head.
We skip and tumble, laughter free,
In every shadow, joy we see.

Laughter Beneath the Pines

Snowflakes dance with glee,
As squirrels trip on trees.
Hot cocoa spills on toes,
While laughter overflows.

Mistakes in the cold air,
Snowmen with goofy hair.
Icicles hang like charms,
Winter's silly alarms.

Hibernating Joys

Bears snooze in cozy beds,
With dreams of honey spreads.
While humans check the fridge,
In search of snacky smidge.

Blankets and pajamas tight,
Chasing socks lost in flight.
We giggle as we flop,
Who knew sleep could be top?

The Color of Frost

Frost paints windows in lace,
As friends join in the race.
Through the chilly delight,
We slip, and all take flight.

Scarves wrapped in knotted cheer,
Snowballs tossed without fear.
Each tumble brings a cheer,
As laughter fills the year.

Soft Shadows in the Snow

Footprints trail in the white,
Kids playing, what a sight!
Snowmen wave like they know,
The fun that steals the show.

In the park, sleds collide,
With giggles that can't hide.
Under stars, we find dreams,
In silly winter themes.

Pine Scented Memories

A tree in the corner, quite tall and round,
With ornaments dangling, oh what a sound!
The cat takes a leap, a crash in the night,
We laugh 'til we cry, what a comical sight!

The smell of pine needles, fresh and so bright,
With cookies and cocoa, we feast with delight.
A squirrel peeks in, thinks it's quite grand,
Not sure it's a friend, but he takes a stand!

Joy Unearthed in Winter's White

Snowflakes come tumbling, a comical dance,
A snowman is built, but it looks like a prance.
Carrot for a nose, and a hat from last year,
He waves as we pass, may he disappear!

Hot cocoa spills over, my hands feel the burn,
Sipping more laughter, oh how it turns!
The snowball brigade starts a fluffy fight,
With giggles and cheers echoing through the night!

Laughter Echoed through the Frost

Frosty the snowman, he's lost his top hat,
Strutting down the street like a fancy old cat.
We join in the chaos, our cheeks all aglow,
In this chilly playground, we run to and fro!

A tumble, a slip, oh we all fall down,
Rolling in the snow, we're the talk of the town.
Then someone yells, 'Snow angel time!'
Covered in white, oh, it's all so sublime!

Serenade of Snowy Whispers

Whispers of snowflakes fall soft on our heads,
The laughter erupts when our sled flies like reds!
We race down the hill, oh what a wild run,
Till someone calls, 'Hey! Why aren't you done?'

The sprites of the winter love playing around,
And leave us with giggles, all merry and sound.
So let's dance with the flakes and sing to the breeze,
In the chorus of laughter, oh, if you please!

Cozy Fireside Tales

By the crackling fire we sit,
Telling stories, never quit.
Socks all mismatched, that's our style,
Laughter echoes, makes us smile.

Hot cocoa spills on the floor,
Sipping loudly, who needs more?
Marshmallows dancing in delight,
Giggles chase the frosty night.

Grandpa's tales of yesteryears,
Involve monsters and some beers.
We all wonder, could it be?
He once wrestled with a tree!

So we raise our mugs and cheer,
For the magic that draws near.
With the snowflakes swirling 'round,
In this warmth, pure joy is found.

Frosted Reveries

The air is crisp, the sky is bright,
Yet sledding down gives us a fright.
We tumble down, all laughter spills,
Like snowflakes falling, such sweet thrills.

The snowman wears my dad's old hat,
With a carrot nose, he looks quite fat.
He starts to melt, but who cares still?
A snack for birds, and all is chill.

Cookies baking, smell so sweet,
We dance around on happy feet.
Then tripping over toys we made,
In wintry magic, we parade.

Under twinkling lights we play,
Whistling tunes that fade away.
With frosted dreams as our guide,
In joyous chaos, we take pride.

The Magic of Winter's Breath

Winter whispers with a grin,
Frozen breath, where do we begin?
Socks are crunching, socks are wet,
On this day, we won't forget.

Snowflakes twirl like ballerinas,
It's a day for silly schemas.
Tangled up, caught in the fun,
As snow fights break, we start to run.

The hot tub steams, oh what a scene,
Wearing hats, it's quite the sheen.
Splashing water, laughter loud,
We invite the snow to join the crowd.

With snowballs flying, giggles rise,
As wintry joy fills up the skies.
In frost and snow, our spirits blend,
This magic breath, we won't pretend.

Hushed Laughter in the Snow

A quiet blanket, white and pure,
Hides the chaos, that's for sure.
We sneak outside, our cheeks aglow,
And tiptoe softly through the snow.

Tiny hedgehogs peek and gawk,
Watch us tumble, frolic, talk.
With whispers soft, we create a plan,
To build a fortress, the biggest, man!

Snowflakes falling, we can't resist,
Patty cakes with frost on our fist.
A chorus sings from trees nearby,
Even branches laugh and sigh.

With frosty noses, joy takes flight,
As starlit magic fills the night.
In every hush and giggled sound,
We find our bliss beneath the ground.

The Lullaby of Ice

Snowflakes dance like clumsy bees,
Falling soft on chill-filled trees.
A penguin slips, with comical flair,
Wobbling round in frosty air.

Hot cocoa spills on mittens bright,
Marshmallows float in a snowy bite.
Giggles echo, in the night's embrace,
As snowmen wear a carrot face.

Icicles hang like frozen art,
Dripping slowly, they play their part.
A snowball fight that turns to glee,
Now who's the snowman? You or me?

So raise a toast with jolly cheer,
To winter's fun, we hold so dear.
With laughter ringing, a joyful sound,
In this frosty world, we dance around.

Frigid Festivities

Socks are stretchy, hats are tight,
Bundled up, we're quite a sight.
Snow boots crunch with every step,
While sledding leads to a laughter prep.

Frosted windows, cheeky views,
Watching squirrels in silly shoes.
They chase their tails with endless glee,
While slipping on a tiny tree.

Cookie dough in snowman shapes,
Baking fails, oh what escapes!
Rolling dough, we start to slide,
In the kitchen, we laugh and hide.

Rooftops covered in blankets white,
With giggly friends, we feel so right.
The chilly air is filled with fun,
As we dash and play 'til day is done.

Gentle Breaths of Frost

Breath like clouds, I puff and blow,
The frosty air, it steals the show.
Chasing snowflakes, I jump and twirl,
While a wayward hat begins to swirl.

Ember glow from fireside cheer,
Fuzzy socks, we're comfy here.
Chess games get loud, with jests that fly,
As snowflakes tumble from a high sky.

Frozen fingers, but hearts are warm,
Bundled hugs, a winter charm.
Giggles bouncing off the walls,
While laughter echoes through the halls.

With hot drinks warming cups in hand,
We brave the snow like a daring band.
Every frosted breath we share,
Is filled with joy and chilled with care.

The Chill of Memories

Winter nights bring tales retold,
Of snowball fights and hearts of gold.
Slipping down the icy lane,
While friends laugh loud through joy and pain.

With stockings hung in crooked rows,
Expecting gifts, the fun just grows.
The mischief of a kitten's pounce,
Causes lopsided laughter to announce.

Tangled lights and marshmallow fights,
We draw the shapes of frosty sights.
Every memory that we keep,
Turns winter nights into giggles deep.

So here's a wink, a joyous cheer,
For every snowy moment here.
With every chill, we find delight,
In laughter shared on a wintry night.

Frosted Branches, Warm Hearts.

Frosted branches, jolly sight,
Squirrels in coats, oh what a fright!
Snowflakes giggle as they fall,
While penguins plot to start a brawl.

Hot cocoa spills, a little clumsy,
Laughter echoes, all feel jumpy.
Nutcrackers dance with wooden style,
As snowmen grin and fake a smile.

Hats are tousled, scarves unwind,
Frosty noses, all snow-blind.
Yet inside, we warm with cheer,
A silly song, the season's near!

Under twinkling lights we chime,
Singing carols, oh so prime.
Oh what joy, in every chill,
We find the fun, and laughter's thrill.

Winter Whispers

Whispers of winter, soft and shrill,
Tell of snowballs, aimed to kill!
Children giggle, cheeks so round,
As they tumble, joy unbound.

Frosty breath in icy air,
Pants on heads without a care.
Snowmen wobble, 'til they drop,
With carrot noses, they won't stop.

Fluffy mittens, mismatched pairs,
Snowboots splash in icy flares.
Giggling hearts, a scene so bright,
In the wonder of frosty light.

Jack Frost tickles sleepy towns,
With chilly fingers, laughter crowns.
Winter's magic, pure delight,
With every giggle, we take flight.

Frost-Kissed Delight

Frost-kissed delight on cheeks so pink,
Teetering snowmen, forming a link.
Hot cider spills, a frosty cue,
While cats in mittens try to chew.

Snowy spectacles, glasses askew,
Felines leap, oh what a view!
Frosty windows, kisses abound,
With giggling groups all gathered round.

Tiny boots leave trails so neat,
While ice skate dancers stomp their feet.
Spinning here, and twirling wide,
Making memories, our hearts collide.

Laughter bubbles like snowflakes spun,
As mischief brews, we all just run.
In the chill, we find our spark,
A winter's tale, igniting the dark.

The Dance of Snowflakes

Snowflakes swirl, in a silly trance,
While mittened hands do a wiggly dance.
Pine trees chuckle, covered in white,
As we prance around, feeling light.

Frosty faces, stuck in glee,
Making snow angels, one, two, three!
Fumbling feet on icy ground,
A slip, a slide, we're heaven-bound.

Chittering friends in woolly hats,
Chasing snowflakes, curious cats.
A snowball fight, what a delight,
With shrieks and giggles, pure revelry tonight.

Under the stars, we shimmy and sway,
Laughing at blunders, come what may.
In every flake that gently falls,
Joy and humor fill our halls.

Shivers of Serenity

The air's a frosty breath,
Snowflakes dance like little sprites,
I slip on ice, but there's no death,
My laughter echoes through the nights.

Hot cocoa spills; oh what a mess,
Marshmallows float like tiny boats,
I tripped again, I must confess,
But joy's the warmth that keeps me afloat.

Socks on hands, hats on my feet,
I waddle like a penguin around,
With frosty noses, we shuffle and greet,
Each giggle sounds like winter's sound.

Candles flicker, shadows play,
The snowman grins with a goofy face,
We throw snowballs, but they stray,
And soon we're in a snowy embrace.

A Chill in the Air

Jackets zipped, but I still shiver,
A squirrel steals my last cookie treat,
I watch him scamper by the river,
While I chase after, quick on my feet.

Frosty air and froth on my lip,
A mug launched, oh what a scene,
With laughter, we take our snowy trip,
Hot chocolate rivers, sledding spree clean.

Snow boots squeak like giggling ducks,
Sleds collide with giggles and shrieks,
The snowball fight brings all the luck,
Until warm mittens make cheeks peak.

Winter games are not so grand,
But every slip brings another cheer,
Embracing cold with a silly hand,
Winter's laughter sings loud and clear.

Embracing the Stillness

Under blankets thick and wide,
I find a friend, my cat astray,
We both snuggle, a furry slide,
While outside children laugh and play.

The snowflakes settle, one by one,
I sip my tea, it warms my soul,
But oops! Down tumbles the honey bun,
Sticky fingers, oh what a goal!

Laughter bubbles like a warm stream,
It's funny how cold can feel so bright,
With silly hats, we drift and dream,
Creating snow angels in moonlight.

A cozy charm in winter's grasp,
As cozy nights drift slow and still,
Each chuckle wrapped in frosty clasp,
This stillness gives a heart a thrill.

Joy Beneath the Stars

Stars twinkle like curious eyes,
I trip on nothing, fall in snow,
The moon laughs; so do my ties,
With every tumble, my joy will grow.

Frost-kissed noses, a glowing cheer,
We chase our shadows, an open lane,
But watch the tree! Oh dear, oh dear!
With snowballs flying, brings only pain.

Scarf wrapped tightly, it's now a race,
More laughter falls than heavy snow,
With goofy hats, we spin and chase,
Our hearts like sleds in the frosty glow.

Beneath the stars, we bounce and slide,
Each joyful chill brings silly laughs,
In winter's dance, we take the ride,
Finding fun in our frozen paths.

A Tapestry of Holiday Wishes

In a land where the snowflakes fall,
Everyone's bundled, chill for all.
Hot cocoa spills from every mug,
Tickling noses with a frosty hug.

Socks are lost in a game of hide,
While snowmen stand with goofy pride.
Caroling echoes, voices stray,
Who knew we all could sing this way?

Mittens clash, mismatched and bright,
Snowball fights with a laugh and slight.
Under streetlights glowing bold,
Jokes are shared as the night grows old.

Laughter dances in the crisp night air,
As friends gather without a care.
Each wish is wrapped with joy and cheer,
Spreading warmth throughout the year.

Where the Air Sings of Snowflakes

The wind whispers tunes that are sweet,
While ice skaters dance on their frosty feet.
Their flailing arms, a sight to behold,
Spinning out stories, both brave and bold.

A squirrel in a hat, oh what a sight,
Chasing his tail in the pale moonlight.
With each slip and slide, giggles abound,
Joy erupts in that snowy playground.

Frosty breath clouds puff in the air,
As friends freeze their toes without a care.
With snowflakes twirl, they join the spree,
Moments like this, so wild and free.

Chill in the air, yet hearts full of glee,
What silliness waits for you and me!
Every laugh shares a warmth so near,
Like hot chocolate's embrace, oh so dear.

Raindrops of Joy on Sledding Hills

Sleds lined up, a chaotic affair,
With giggles echoing everywhere.
One brave soul takes the first bold ride,
Flying through snow, arms open wide.

A tumble here, a spin, oh my!
Snowflakes catch as we all fly high.
Laughter mixes with the chilly breeze,
As cheeks grow red like roasty peas.

Hot tamales from the food stand nearby,
Piping hot, oh me, oh my!
The air's alive with games and cheer,
Each brave soul finds their winter gear.

In a world of white, let's just play,
With snowmen crafting a funny way.
Each raindrop of joy brings us near,
To a season that sings, so crystal clear.

The Warmth Within the Cold

Under blankets piled high with cheer,
We tell tales of snowmen cozy here.
With mugs in hand, marshmallows float,
Each story shared earns a gloating note.

Crackling fires and glowing lights,
As we debate our snowball fights.
In this warmth, we jest and tease,
With each chilly bite, we laugh with ease.

Slippers squeaking upon the floor,
As relatives bust through the door.
Their wild tales of snow and more,
Bring laughter that we can't ignore.

So let's shout out a merry sound,
For joy in cold is all around.
In every chuckle, a secret told,
Finding warmth within, pure as gold.

Chilly Embraces

Frosty noses, cheeks so red,
Snowflakes stick upon my head.
Penguins waddle, kids throw snow,
All this joy, where did it go?

Snowmen dance with floppy hats,
But they melt—oh silly rats!
Sleds go flying, laughter roars,
Until we crash, then roll on floors.

Hot cocoa spills, we laugh and sigh,
"Why is it cold?" I boldly cry.
Yet here we are, in snowball fights,
With frozen mittens, scaling heights.

Wrap me tight in blankets, please,
I'll share this chill with all my knees!
For every giggle, shiver, and cheer,
Winter's punchline—we hold dear!

Dreams in White

Under blankets, warm and tight,
I dream of snowmen made of night.
The stars in their frosty wrappings hide,
While I, awake, wear socks with pride.

Slippers squeak on icy floor,
I make a dash, then sprint to the door.
Snowflakes tickle as I shout,
"Who's the best at winter clout?"

Cats and dogs, they leap and play,
Chasing tails throughout the day.
Caught in snowdrifts, they look so smug,
Nature's jester, cozy in a rug.

So let it snow, let laughter reign,
In this wild world, we're all insane.
We'll dance in flakes, a giddy pirouette,
And in our dreams, we'll never forget!

The Canvas of Winter

A canvas white, a playful shift,
Balloons afloat, they make me lift.
Carefree spirits, oh what a sight,
Painting laughter in pure delight.

Ice skates gliding, oh so bold,
With epic spills, our stories told.
Snowflakes twirl like champions grand,
Each one a giggle, like merry band.

Hot stew bubbles, the kitchen's glow,
While snowflakes outside put on a show.
Fumbling mittens, coffee spills,
It's all a joy; it gives me chills!

As nightfall blankets this snowy spree,
Hot cocoa smiles and laughter decree.
The world may freeze, but our hearts will warm,
In this silly season, we find our charm.

Twinkling Starlight

Underneath the twinkling glow,
Frosty stars in lights do flow.
Reindeer prancing, silly sleigh,
Dashing through in a quirky way.

The moon is laughing, oh so bright,
As snowflakes fall in sheer delight.
Unruly mittens and runaway hats,
All make for priceless winter chats.

With snowball armies on the prowl,
We launch our dreams, like a happy growl.
But all is well, no need for fear,
As laughter echoes, loud and clear.

So gather 'round, let stories fly,
In merry warmth, beneath the sky.
While starlit dreams twinkle above,
We share the joy, wrapped in love!

Frostbitten Lullabies

Snowflakes dance like crazy gnomes,
Whispering secrets in winter homes.
Hot cocoa spills on mittens bright,
Grandpa snores with delight each night.

Socks pulled high, a festive sight,
Tangled lights give cats a fright.
Penguins slide on frosty ground,
While children giggle all around.

Icicles hang like disco balls,
Nature's laughter in chilly calls.
Snowmen sport a carrot nose,
As winter's antics freely flow.

Slipping, sliding, oh what fun!
Sledding races, who has won?
Frostbitten toes, can't feel a thing,
Let's toast to the joy this season brings!

The Hidden Joy Beneath the Ice

Under layers of frozen delight,
Lies a secret, swirling tight.
Skaters glide with comic grace,
Winter's dance, an awkward race.

Snowball fights with sneaky spry,
Facepalms in the snow, oh my!
Every tumble brings a cheer,
Frozen laughter that we hear.

In the thump of snowflakes' fall,
Epic fails, we'll have a ball.
Frosty noses, cheeks aglow,
With snowmen that look like they know.

Beneath the ice, a warm embrace,
Magic moments fill the space.
With every chuckle, every grin,
Winter's fun has just begun!

A Palette of Holiday Hues

Crimson bows on frozen pines,
Twinkling lights dance like designs.
Cinnamon sticks and cookie dough,
Images of joy, all aglow.

Socks and mittens, oh so bright,
Fashion statements in the night.
Grandma's laughter fills the air,
With a wink and an icy stare.

Mittens missing, where are they?
Furry friends run off to play.
Scarf wrapped tight, just like a hug,
Winter warmth, snug as a bug.

Each color shines, a jolly scene,
With all the laughter in between.
The palette blooms with winter cheer,
Who knew fun could persevere?

Candles Flicker in the Crisp Night

Candles glow like tiny stars,
Casting shadows, dancing far.
Hot cider sips with spice around,
While we laugh without a sound.

Frosty windows, drawings made,
Reindeer leaping, unafraid.
Lost mittens found in potpourri,
Winter's charm, pure jubilee.

Each little spark ignites a thrill,
As snowflakes fall with gentle chill.
A cozy scene, not too tight,
With jokes and pranks all through the night.

As frosty breezes gently sigh,
Whimsical laughter fills the sky.
With every flicker, joy ignites,
In playful warmth of cold winter nights!

Cheer in the Frost

Frosty noses meet with glee,
Hot cocoa spills, oh woe is me!
Snowflakes dance like they're on a spree,
Slipping, sliding, what a sight to see!

Scarves wrapped tight, we're all a mess,
Laughter reigns, I must confess.
Snowballs fly, no time to stress,
Who knew cold could bring such zest?

Kids in sleds zoom past with cheer,
Chasing dogs, they disappear.
Footprints tell tales of frolic and cheer,
Winter's antics, we hold dear!

Hot soup warms from head to toe,
Outside we play, not wanting to go.
Winter's magic, what a show,
We chuckle as snowmen grow!

The Sparkle of Quiet Nights

Stars twinkle high, what a delight,
We chase shadows in the soft moonlight.
Snowflakes land like feathers so white,
Sipping laughter as the world feels right.

Muted whispers, snow covers the ground,
A giggle here, it's a joyous sound.
Midwinter mischief, look all around,
Frozen chuckles in silence abound.

Cocoa mustaches on everyone's lips,
Avoiding frost on our funny trips.
With mittened hands and joyful quips,
We dance away on slippery slips!

Barking dogs join in the embrace,
Rolling snowballs is quite the race.
Even the cat joins this playful chase,
Winter's magic puts smiles on every face!

Flurries of Joy

Little flakes tumble from the sky,
Children scream and start to fly.
Snowmen wobble, oh me, oh my,
Laughter rings, no one knows why!

Frost on eyebrows, what a sight,
Running around, hearts take flight.
Under the streetlamp, it feels so bright,
Snowball fights turn into delight!

The baker's kitchen, sweet treats abound,
Cookies vanish without a sound.
Pies like mountains are set unbound,
Who knew joy could spin round and round?

Frosty fingers, noses aglow,
Stumbling home, all moving slow.
With giggles shared and voices that flow,
Falling in love with the winter show!

The Art of Frosted Moments

Tiny ponies made of snow,
Chasing giggles as we go.
Arctic winds with a playful blow,
Winter's canvas, all aglow!

Puddle splashes, oops, a flop,
Cuddly hats we never stop.
Friendly laughter makes us hop,
It's an art, oh, what a crop!

Candied apples, sticky sweet,
Winter recipes, a tasty treat.
Baking with friends, oh what a feat,
In the kitchen, fun can't be beat!

Joyful messes, all over the floor,
Ice-skating trips, laughter galore.
Wrapped in warmth, who could want more?
In frosted moments, our hearts soar!

A Chill Amidst the Cheer

Snowflakes dance upon my nose,
Tickling me from head to toes.
Hot cocoa spills upon my shirt,
Ah, the joys of winter dirt!

Frosty breath like dragon's puff,
Wooly hats can't be too plush.
We stumble, slip, and laugh some more,
Who knew ice could be such a chore!

Giant snowmen blocking the way,
With carrots that want to play.
They wobble, giggle, and tip on down,
Each tumble brings a snowy crown!

So let's embrace this frosty glee,
Winter's quirks are fun, you see.
With each laugh and icy spill,
We find joy in each winter thrill!

Glittering Holidays

Tinsel thrown like spaghetti strands,
The cat's caught in the festive bands.
Ornaments are all out of place,
Where did I leave the pie, oh grace!

Twinkling lights spark in delight,
But tangled cords steal the night.
Cookies eaten, crumbs in a trail,
Just one more snack, I won't fail!

Sledding down the hill we glide,
Whoops! There goes my mitten's ride.
Laughter echoes in the air,
Who knew winter's fun could scare!

So raise a cup, let's toast and cheer,
To the silly moments, every year.
Joy wraps around us like a scarf,
In this frosty, giggly heart's hearth!

Faraway Frost

Frosty windows, a painting surreal,
What's outside? Just some snowy wheal.
The snowman grins, a cheeky chap,
As he hides my sled in his lap!

Penguins waddling on the floor,
Why are their snacks by the door?
With jokes that tickle my frosty toes,
I chase after winter, as laughter flows!

Icicles dangled like sharp teeth,
Where did my mittens take their leave?
Hilarity ensues, as I fall flat,
Puffing like a snowball cat!

Snowball fights that miss their aim,
I fear I've lost this silly game.
Yet in this chill, we find the fun,
With each slip, a new joke spun!

Whimsy in Winter

Snowflakes fall with a chuckle and grin,
While squirrels gather in a winterly din.
They bury nuts like treasure astir,
But find them lost in a pile of fur!

Carrot noses on each snowball we toss,
Oops, my hat has gone — what a loss!
The fun is endless in this white maze,
Every slip brings a frosty praise!

Hot chocolate dribbles, oh what a sight,
Marshmallows dancing in the night.
If laughter's the goal in this snowy spree,
Let's roll and tumble, just you and me!

The chilly air sings a humorous song,
Follow the giggles, where we belong.
In this winter wonderland, bright and bold,
We weave our stories, forever told!

Magical Nights of Silk and Snow

In the air, a flurry flits,
Snowflakes dance like little skits.
Socks are warm, mittens tight,
Snowballs fly with pure delight.

Giggling under a bright moon's glow,
Winter's laugh, a radiant show.
Hot cocoa spills, a frothy prize,
Marshmallows swim, oh what a surprise!

Frosty trees wear crystal bling,
As laughter floats and children sing.
Sledding down with squeals of glee,
Watch out! Here comes another spree!

Candles flicker in cozy nooks,
Storytime with giggly looks.
In a quilt of wonder we remain,
Warmth and laughter like a train.

Joyride down the Ice-coated Lane

Beneath the stars, we speed along,
Skates, not wheels, let's prove them wrong.
Neighbors watch, with jaws agape,
As we twist and twirl, a frosty capes.

One slip, and off goes my hat,
"Oh look! A penguin skidded flat!"
Laughter rings through the chilly night,
As we conquer this skating flight.

Hot dogs steaming by the old post,
Catch them quick, it's a winter toast!
Ketchup squirts with a happy cheer,
Taste the joy, it's the best time of year!

Passing reindeer in a sleigh,
They nod and wink, they join the play.
Rolling home with cheeks aglow,
What a ride in the frost and flow!

Sweet Surprises Under Frosty Canopies

Under the trees, where snowflakes hide,
We dance and fall, our laughter wide.
Candy canes and baked delights,
Frost your nose with chilly bites.

Surprises wait, wrapped up tight,
Beneath the bow and twinkly light.
"Is that a gift? Oh, what's inside?"
A whirling cookie we can't abide!

Gifts that slip and prankish sighs,
A jolly snowman grins, oh my!
With frosty breath, we make a plan,
To sneak a hug, and there we ran!

Hot chocolate flows from magic pots,
With whipped cream swirls and smiling spots.
Together we dance, together we soar,
In a world where silly dreams explore.

The Chill of Togetherness

Gather round in the winter's hold,
With stories shared, we break the cold.
Blankets piled, cocoa warm,
Each little heart is safe from harm.

A tickle fight sends giggles high,
As snowmen watch us from nearby.
Frosty jokes and silly pranks,
Life is grand, we give our thanks!

Carols sung, a choir of laughs,
Mittens paired and splitting halves.
Snowflakes crash on the windowpanes,
Yet warmth is here, it still remains.

Together, we cheer, swap tales of old,
With chilly fingers, love is bold.
In the night, our spirits lift,
Together we found the greatest gift.

Heartfelt Snowfall

Snowflakes dance and swirl so high,
A squirrel slips and says 'Oh my!'
With cocoa mugs in mittened hands,
We build a snowman—he understands.

Laughter echoes in the white,
He shivers but holds on tight.
While snowballs fly through the air,
I duck and hide—if I dare.

Frosty noses, cheeks so red,
A race to warm up in my bed!
But oh, those footprints in the snow,
Lead to the cookie stash, you know!

So here's to frosty, funny days,
In this winter wonderland maze!
With sleds and giggles all around,
Joy in every snowy mound.

Bright Lights Against the Frost

Twinkling bulbs on every street,
Ice skaters dance with frozen feet.
A snowman wears a goofy hat,
While penguins waddle—imagine that!

Hot chocolate spills, oh what a sight!
The dog slips too—what a delight!
We sing carols off-key and loud,
Each note dissolves into the crowd.

From chilly airs, warm laughter peaks,
Socks that stink are what we seek.
In woolly sweaters, we all misfit,
Yet warmth and love is truly lit.

As chilly nights create their charm,
We squeeze our friends—we mean no harm!
With lights aglow and gingerbread,
Oh, the shenanigans we spread!

Cherished Memories in the Chill

Snow forts rise like castles tall,
A mitten-sharp snowball to my pal.
With each tackle and tumble around,
We roll and laugh upon the ground.

Gingerbread houses, icing sweets,
My dog sneaks in, and everyone cheered!
As we trim the tree, tangled lights,
'Tis the season for silly fights!

Then comes the joy of cozy nights,
Fluffy slippers and fireplace lights.
The cat climbs high in her new fort,
As we gather close for a fun sport.

So here we are in laughter's embrace,
Tip-toeing through this enchanting space.
Memories made, so warm and bright,
Under the stars—what a sight!

Enchanted Evening Snows

The moon hangs low, snow drapes the town,
A reindeer cheers as he fumbles down.
With boots that squeak on the icy floor,
We slide, we laugh, we always want more!

The holiday lights twinkle so bright,
Turning the dark into sheer delight.
As snowflakes fall in a whirl and spin,
We build snow angels and jump right in!

A party of mittens, we sip and cheer,
Out in the cold, we have no fear.
With friends and snacks, all bundled tight,
Winter's a joy, pure fun at night!

So here's the magic that each year brings,
Stories of laughter and the joy it sings.
In this frosty fun, let us take flight,
Together we'll dance in the shimmering light!

Winter's Embrace

Snowflakes dance with glee,
As we slip on icy tea.
Scarves wrapped like a hug,
Falling fast, like a bug.

Hot cocoa in hand,
Laughs echo across the land.
With noses red and bright,
Snowmen wobble in delight.

Sleds fly with giddy grace,
A tumble, then a race.
Frosty breath in play,
Who needs the sun, anyway?

And when the day is done,
Our cheeks rosy from the fun.
We'll dream of snowy days,
And giggle in frosty ways.

The Warmth of Laughter

Chilly air, cheeks aglow,
With epic snowball throws!
Laughter's warmth fills the air,
While hats fly without a care.

Bundled up like a roast,
Neighbors toast to the most!
Hot pies serve with a grin,
Socks mismatched; let the fun begin!

Dancing in a snow suit,
With penguin moves that are cute.
One leg's down, one's in flight,
Turns out, ice is not just white!

Gathered round the fire's light,
Tales get taller every night.
Winter brings us all together,
Joy wrapped in this cold weather.

Glistening Icicles

Icicles hang like teeth,
Dripping water underneath.
A stumbling cat on ice,
Prancing round, oh so nice!

We watch them glisten bright,
With giggles that take flight.
A snowball hits the tree,
"Did that squirrel just throw me?"

Snow forts rise with pride,
Children play side by side.
Each flake a tiny clown,
As they tumble, fall down.

Under the moon's soft glow,
Maxing out on melt and snow.
With every chill and thrill,
Winter's games give quite a thrill!

Whispers Beneath the Snow

The world whispers and sighs,
As frosty breath fills the skies.
Under blankets piled high,
Hot tea flows; oh my, oh my!

Every crunch is a song,
Telling tales where we belong.
Snowmen plotting at night,
With carrot noses, what a sight!

Footprints lead to mischief,
Tracing paths with a stiff whiff.
A slippery dance, oh what fun,
Twisting round, 'til we're done!

When the days feel so cold,
And stories of fun unfold.
We gather, hearts warm and wide,
In winter's joy, we abide.

Songs of the Snowfall

Snowflakes dance and twirl around,
Making all the laughter sound.
Sleds go flying, kids take flight,
Even snowmen wear a smile so bright.

Hot cocoa spills, marshmallows fly,
As snowballs soar up to the sky.
Each yelp and giggle fills the air,
Winter's a joke that's hard to bear.

Gloves are tangled, hats go stray,
"Whose sled is that?" we shout in play.
Snow forts built with such great pride,
Then attacked by kids, oh what a ride!

Snowy days bring such delight,
With snowmen wobbling left and right.
We laugh until our cheeks turn red,
And dream of warmer days instead.

Warm Hearts in the Cold

Bundled up in layers thick,
Searching for a snowball trick.
Winter breathes in funny sights,
As noses freeze and shivers bite.

Hot soup spills, a playful fight,
We chase our scarves with sheer delight.
Fingers numb, we still must try,
To catch a snowflake with a sigh.

Outside we stumble, slippered feet,
A frosty slip can't be beat!
With jolly laughter, we collide,
In the snowy world, we take our stride.

Mom's cookies lure, the warmth inside,
While snowmen watch, all full of pride.
Around the fire, we swap our tales,
Of snowy days and epic fails.

A Winter's Palette

Painted skies of gray and white,
We sled down hills with sheer delight.
Snowball fights, we plot and scheme,
Frosty air and a winter dream.

Laughter erupts with every fall,
Teetering on the edge of a wall.
Mittens lost in a snowy spree,
Making memories wild and free.

The world outside is crisp and clean,
With every flake, the joy is seen.
We build snow castles, grand and tall,
Then watch them crumble with snowball brawl.

With hot drinks and laughter's cheer,
Every winter brings us near.
A palette of joy, so bright and bold,
In the chilly tales, we love retold.

Frosty Frolics

Frosted windows and giggling crowds,
Wrapped up tight, a sea of shrouds.
We dash outside with squeals of glee,
No time to waste, so wild and free.

Toboggans flying, twirling wide,
Watch out! Here comes a slippery slide!
Snowflakes tickle, laughter rings,
In this chill, joy truly springs.

Ice skates on and off we go,
Chasing friends in a frosty show.
Slips and trips, a comic scene,
In this winter wonder, life's a dream.

Hot drinks waiting, tales to share,
Warm hearts beating, joy in the air.
With frosty fun and spirits high,
We turn each snow day into a pie!

Heartwarming Winter Tales

Snowflakes softly twirl in air,
Hot cocoa spills, we laugh and care.
A snowman wobbles, he can't stand,
His carrot nose fell, oh how bland!

Wind's a prankster, whispers 'boo!',
It tugs at hats, it plays peek-a-boo.
We chase our mittens, wrapped in fun,
With every slip, we laugh and run!

Icicles hang like crooked teeth,
The dog leaps high, he's a snow wreath.
We slide on ice, oh what a sight,
As snowballs soar, we're lost in flight!

Morning frost coats trees with bling,
In fluffy boots, we dance and sing.
We belly flop on snowy hills,
With rosy cheeks, we chase the thrills!

Glowing Lanterns in the Chill

Lanterns glow like fireflies bright,
We trip on shadows in the night.
Furry hats with pom-poms dance,
A snowball skirmish leads to a prance!

Frosty breath like tiny clouds,
We giggle loud in bundled crowds.
A squirrel suits up for a game,
He's got acorns, oh what a claim!

The ice rink's calling, with a slide,
Skates on, we twirl, our grace a ride.
But whoops! The laughter paints the air,
As flailing arms end in a scare!

Jingle bells ring through the chill,
As gingerbread men race downhill.
We set our sights on sugar heights,
With cheeky grins and snowy bites!

Frosted Joy and Wonder

Frosted windows show our glee,
We sip on cheer with glee-filled tea.
A pie so flaky, oh so fine,
Mom says, 'Save some, it's divine!'

We bundle up, it's quite the scene,
In mismatched socks, we strut like queens.
A dance-off starts, we shimmy tight,
The dog joins in, a furry delight!

Jumps in puddles, splashes fly,
But one big splash gets in my eye!
A laugh erupts, we roll in snow,
With chilly noses, the fun won't slow!

Snow days bring the best of times,
With friendly barks and silly rhymes.
We make our forts, defend with flair,
With giggles echoing everywhere!

Silvery Dreams

Under moonlight, snowflakes shine,
We make our wishes, dreams align.
A twinkling star begins to play,
The night is silly, come what may!

Angels made from drifts of white,
We laugh at shapes, what a sight!
In cozy blankets, stories flow,
While outside dances winter's show.

The warmth of hugs and jokes exchanged,
In frosty air, our hearts unchained.
A snickering snowman sneaks behind,
With laughter shared, our souls entwined!

With every step, the world aglow,
We spin and twirl in flakes that flow.
In this brisk dance, our spirits lift,
In chilly joy, we find our gift!

Milton Keynes UK
Ingram Content Group UK Ltd.
UKHW020046271124
451585UK00012B/1083